KILLER WHALES

The Orcas of the Pacific Ocean

by *Nancy J. Nielsen*

Illustrated with photographs
by Jeff Jacobsen
and the Marine Mammal Fund

Reading consultant:

John Manning, Professor of Reading, University of Minnesota

D0103515

Capstone Press

MINNEAPOLIS

Capstone Press • 2440 Fernbrook Lane • Minneapolis, MN 55447

Editorial Director   John Coughlan
Managing Editor   John Martin
Copy Editor   Gil Chandler

Library of Congress Cataloging-in-Publication Data

Nielsen, Nancy J.
  Killer Whales / by Nancy J. Nielsen; photographs by Jeff
  Jacobsen and the Marine Mammal Fund.
     p. cm.--
  Includes bibliographical references and index.
  ISBN 1-56065-236-5 (lib. bdg.)
  1. Killer whale--Juvenile literature. 2. Killer whale--Behavior-
  -Juvenile literature. 3. Whales [1. Killer whale.]
I. Jacobsen, Jeff, ill. II. Marine Mammal Fund. III. Title.
QL737.C432N55   1995
599.5'3--dc20   94-27963
                                                    CIP
                                                    AC
ISBN: 1-56065-236-5

99 98 97 96 95 94   8 7 6 5 4 3 2 1

Acknowledgments

The author thanks: The Center for Whale Research; Gerard Gormley, author of *Orcas of the Gulf: A Natural History* and *A Dolphin Summer*; and The Whale Museum, Friday Harbor, Washington.

Table of Contents

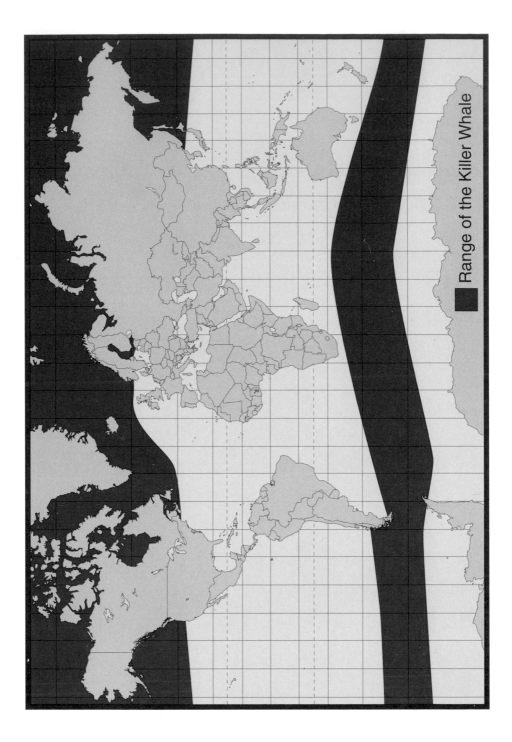

Range of the Killer Whale

Facts about Killer Whales

Scientific name: *Orcinus Orca*

Description:

Length: Males grow to 30 feet (9 meters), females reach lengths of 23 feet (7 meters).

Weight: Males grow to 8 tons (7,256 kilograms), females are as large as 6 tons (5,443 kilograms).

Physical features: A blowhole on top of its head, small eyes, about 50 teeth, and a powerful tail.

Colors: Black and white.

Distinctive habits: Must leave the water to breathe. They travel in groups and are able to communicate with one another.

Food: Fish, seals, dolphins, sea lions.

Reproduction: Females give birth to only one calf every 4 to 6 years. Occasionally, twins may be born.

Life span: 50 to 80 years.

Range: Worldwide.

Habitat: Cold coastal waters.

Chapter 1

Killer Appetites

When scientists opened up a dead killer whale, they found the bodies of 13 dolphins and 15 adult seals in its stomach. In another killer whale they found the bodies of 3 sea lions and 17 adult seals.

Killer whales–also known as orcas–have great appetites. They eat squid, sharks, seals, and sea lions. They eat walruses and porpoises. They even eat whales larger than themselves.

A killer whale swims near a group of sea lions, who wisely stay on shore.

A killer whale pounces on a sea lion as blood spreads through the water.

Fierce and intelligent predators, killer whales often hunt in groups, like wolves and lions. They are the most feared of all the ocean's creatures–that's why they're called killer whales.

Grabbing Sea Lions

A hungry killer whale swims near a beach in Argentina. She knows that sea lions are on the beach. When a young sea lion strays from the group, the whale goes into action. She dives hard against the waves and steers toward shore with her powerful tail.

The whale grabs the sea lion just as she slides onto the beach. For a moment her giant body lies still. With the next wave, she wiggles loose and floats back to deeper waters.

There she tosses the young sea lion into the air several times. Then she shares the tasty treat with the other whales in her **pod**.

Going after Seals

In the Arctic Ocean, two young whales spot a seal on a piece of ice. One whale suddenly dives under the ice, then lifts it with his huge body. The seal slides into the waiting jaws of the other hunter.

Food—and Lots of It

Killer whales are expert and ferocious hunters. Because food is scarce and their appetites are large, they have to spend about half of their time hunting for food.

An adult orca needs from 55 to 175 pounds (25 to 80 kilograms) of food a day. A killer whale that feeds on salmon needs about 20 to 25 fish a day. A seal-hunting orca has to catch one baby seal a day. If she shares it with the other whales in her pod, she will need to catch more.

Chapter 2

The Killer Whale or Orca

The killer whale's scientific name is *Orcinus orca*. They are **mammals** and are the largest members of a family of whales known as *Delphinidae*, which includes the smaller toothed whales known as dolphins.

A Smaller Whale

Adult male killer whales weigh about eight tons (7,213 kilograms). Adult females weigh about a third less than the males–five or six tons (4,535 or 5,443 kilograms). This is small for a whale. Compare the orca to the blue whale, the largest whale, which weighs as much as 120 tons (108,000 kilograms).

At Home in All Oceans

Killer whales are found in all the oceans of the world. They live in coastal waters and in the deepest ocean far from land. They seem to prefer colder waters within 500 miles (800 kilometers) of shore.

Toothed Whales

Killer whales are toothed whales. They have from 44 to 48 teeth. Each tooth is about an inch (2.5 centimeters) wide and as long as your finger.

Killer whales use their teeth only to grasp and tear their prey. They don't chew their food. They swallow their meals whole.

Eyes and Ears

The orca has two eyes, one on each side of its head. The whale can see underwater and above the surface.

The orca has two ears as well, one above each eye. Its ears are inner ears, deep in its head. A small opening is all that can be seen.

Coloring

The killer whale's black-and-white coloring makes it easy to identify. Its back and sides are black, and its underside is white. It has a patch of white shaped like a teardrop above and behind each eye.

The two colors help to **camouflage** the whale. Its prey cannot see that the two colors actually make one huge killer until it's too late.

Flippers, Flukes, and Dorsal Fin

A killer whale's **flippers** are large, rounded fins shaped like paddles. They help it balance and steer through the water. The killer whale's flippers are large–as long as six feet or more (two meters) and as wide as four feet (1.2 meters).

Its tail has two fins called **flukes**. The flukes of an adult male may be as large as nine feet (2.7 meters) across. The whale moves these up and down as it swims.

Another fin, the **dorsal fin**, sticks out of the water when the whale swims close to the surface. In male killer whales, this fin may be as tall as six

feet (1.8 meters). It is somewhat smaller in female whales.

The Saddle Patch

Behind the dorsal fin on the whale's back is a grey patch. This is called the saddle patch. Because each whale's saddle patch is different, scientists use the patches to tell one whale from another.

The grey patch behind the dorsal fins of killer whales helps researchers identify them.

Chapter 3

Swimming and Breathing

Killer whales are among the fastest swimmers in the ocean. They can swim as fast as 30 miles (48 kilometers) per hour. They have a cruising speed of 2 to 5 miles (3.2 to 8 kilometers) per hour.

Killer whales are easy to recognize by the way they swim. They make three to five short dips under water, 10 to 30 seconds apart. Then they dive for three or four minutes.

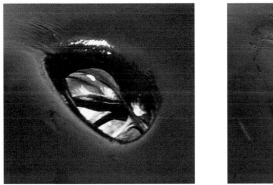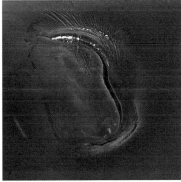

On the surface, whales breathe out through the blowhole *(left)*, but close the blowhole when they swim underwater *(right)*.

Breathing through a Blowhole

Like all mammals, a killer whale has to hold its breath when it swims underwater. It can hold its breath for as long as 20 minutes if necessary.

When it comes to the surface, it blows the old air out of a **blowhole** in the top of its head. The blowing makes a loud, deep sound–whuff!   The plume of water it blows is from 5 to 15 feet (1.5 to 4.5 meters) high.   The whale takes a new

breath and then closes the blowhole before diving
again.

Breaching

Killer whales sometimes leap out of the water
in a spectacular way. This is called breaching.

A killer whale falls backward after breaching.

They may do this to communicate with other whales, or to shake off parasites, or maybe just to maintain their strength.

Chapter 4

Pods

Killer whales live together in family groups called pods. These groups can have as few as five or as many as 50 or more whales in them. The whales in a pod help each other, hunt together, and work together to protect their young.

The oldest female orca leads the pod. She may live for 50 to 80 years. (Male orcas live shorter lives–usually fewer than 50 years.) The leader's children live in the pod with her. They usually stay with their mother when they become adults.

Resident Pods

Some pods are resident pods. These stay in the same location most of the time. The largest killer whale pods are resident pods. Scientists think that these pods eat mostly fish.

Transient Pods

Other pods are transient pods. These are smaller groups of five or so whales that travel over much greater distances. They eat mostly seals and other whales.

Chapter 5

Mating, Giving Birth, and Growing Up

Orcas can mate when they are in their middle teens, but they don't reach their full size until they are in their late teens. They often mate in the late spring and early summer months but can mate at any time of the year. A whale always mates with a whale from another pod.

The male and female whales do not stay together after mating. The mother takes care of any **offspring** that result from mating.

Giving Birth

Orca mothers usually give birth for the first time when they are 14 or 15 years old. They give birth once every 3 to 10 years and usually have only one calf at a time.

A pregnancy lasts 13 to 16 months. Most births occur in the fall and early winter. At birth, killer whale calves weigh 400 pounds (180 kilograms) and are seven to eight feet (2.1 to 2.4 meters) long.

If a female whale is about to give birth, the other whales in her pod will help her. When the calf slides out of the mother, another whale brings the calf to the surface so it can breathe.

The calf soon learns to breathe without help. Then it finds its mother's teat and begins to **suckle**–to feed on its mother's milk.

Growing Up

Every pod member helps to protect the calf. When the baby stops to drink its mother's milk, the other whales slow down to watch for danger.

If a mother whale goes off to hunt, young whales babysit the calf until the mother returns.

Baby whales are often playful. When a big orca comes up for air, a calf will lie on its head and try to cover its blowhole. The adult playfully dumps the baby off.

Sleeping

When baby whales are not eating or playing, they sleep. Sometimes the entire pod sleeps together. When killer whales sleep they take deep breaths and then rest just below the surface of the water. Every three minutes or so they wake up. They come to the surface to breathe and then sink back into the waves for another short nap.

Chapter 6
Communicating

ReeeEEE, ReeeeeeeEEEEEEE! Whaaaaa-eeeee-aaaaa-eeeee-aaaaa! Unnnnooooooo! Zweeeeeeeeep! Aaaaaauuup!

Killer whales are talking to each other. One sound may signal danger. Another may tell that a large prey has been found. When one pod of whales meets another pod, the whales greet each other with high-pitched sounds.

Each pod has calls that only the whales of that pod make. The calls help the whales of a pod keep track of each other. Because an orca will mate only with a member of a different pod, the sounds also may help a whale find a mate.

Other Ways of Communicating

Killer whales also make a clicking sound. Many of these clicks, close together, make a creaking or buzzing sound. The clicks travel through the water and echo back off a rock or an animal. They tell the orca the location and size of the rock or animal.

The clicks help the orcas "see" underwater. The whale uses the mound of fat on its head, called a melon, to focus the echoing sounds. This ability is called **echolocation**.

Communicating with Humans

Orcas also communicate with humans. A pod of whales once followed a group of scientists for several weeks. Sometimes the pod allowed them to come near. But one day a big male splashed the boat with his huge flukes. The scientists understood the splash to mean "Stay away! You're getting too close." They quickly moved their boat away.

Chapter 7

Killer Whales and the Environment

A large oil tanker is sailing near Alaska. It hits a rock, and a jagged hole opens in the side of the ship. Oil spills into the ocean, forming a black, oily slick. A pod of killer whales swims through the slick. Oil covers the whales, getting into their mouths and blowholes.

Six days after the spill, scientists who had been studying the pod found seven whales missing. Because orcas rarely leave their pods, and a pod usually loses only one or two whales a year, scientists think the missing whales died from the oil.

Even if the whales do survive a spill, the oil will destroy their food. Killer whales eat both fish and mammals. They are at the top of the ocean's **food chain**. Many small animals feed on **plankton**. Fish eat these small animals, and then dolphins and sea lions feed on the fish. When oil destroys one link in the food chain, killer whales have nothing to eat.

Protecting the Orcas

Killer whales are not yet **endangered**. There are great numbers of them throughout the world. Some scientists studying orcas off Antarctica estimate that there are 160,000 killer whales in just that area alone.

There are rules and laws to protect orcas from humans. Boats, which can hurt the whales with their propellers, must stay at least 100 yards (91.4 meters) away from the whales. They must approach the whales slowly and are not allowed to chase them.

Chapter 8

Killer Whales in Captivity

In 1965, Ted Griffin heard that a killer whale had been snared in a fishing net. Ted bought the whale and moved it to his marine park in Seattle.

Would It Work?

No one knew how a killer whale would act in captivity. Ted was surprised to see that the whale was friendly and seemed to like humans.

Ted named the whale Namu. Namu learned tricks and even let Ted ride on his back.

Ted grew fond of the whale. But Namu died after being in captivity for only 11 months. The water in his pen had become polluted. Ted decided it was better to let killer whales live on their own in the ocean.

An Orca Movie Star

In the movie *Free Willy*, a young boy becomes friends with a killer whale who lives at a marine park. The boy realizes that the whale can hear his pod calling to him from the ocean. He helps the whale return to the wild.

The whale who starred in the movie is named Keiko. He now lives in Mexico City at Reino Aventura, a marine park. His pool is much too small for him. His dorsal fin droops from lack of exercise. He is underweight and has a rash. His gums are sore and his teeth have worn down from gnawing on the side of the pool.

Some people think Keiko should be freed. Others say that he is too sick to be able to hunt in the open ocean.

Caring for Killer Whales

There are now about 45 killer whales in captivity. Trainers are learning how to care for them. Sea World in California, for example, has built large saltwater pools. Several whales can live there together.

In marine parks, scientists can observe killer whales up close. They can learn some things about orcas that they would never learn from studying them in the wild.

There are many things we still do not know about killer whales. With time, we will learn more about the role these fascinating animals play in the life of the oceans.

Glossary

baleen–the narrow plates extending from the upper jaw of some whales, used to strain water

blowhole–the opening on a whale's head through which it breathes

blubber–a thick layer of fat under the skin of a whale

camouflage–a color pattern that helps an animal to hide itself by blending into its surroundings

dorsal fin–the narrow section of skin that rises from a whale's back and helps it steer through the water

echolocation–the system of finding and measuring objects by bouncing sounds off them and listening to the echo

endangered–to be threatened by extinction

flippers–large, rounded fins that help a whale steer through the water

flukes–two fins that lie on either side of the whale's tail. The flukes move up and down as the whale swims.

food chain–the system of feeding in an ecosystem, in which a larger species eats smaller ones

offspring–the children of an animal

plankton–small organisms that float in the water and which fish feed on

pod–a group of killer whales that live together

suckle–to feed on milk from a mother's breast

To Learn More

Arnold, Caroline. *Killer Whale*. New York: Morrow, 1994.

Gormley, Gerard. *Orcas of the Gulf: A Natural History*. San Francisco: Sierra Club, 1990.

Heimlich-Boran, Sara and James Heimlich-Boran. *Killer Whales*. Stillwater, MN: Voyageur, 1994.

Leon, Vicki. *A Pod of Killer Whales*. San Luis Obispo, CA: Blake, 1989.

Patent, Dorothy Hinshaw. *Killer Whales*. New York: Holiday House, 1993.

Simon, Seymour. *Killer Whales*. Philadelphia: Lippincott, 1978.

Stephens, William M. and Peggy Stephens. *Killer Whale: Mammal of the Sea*. New York, Holiday House, 1971.

Waters, John F. *Watching Whales*. New York: Cobblehill Books, 1991.

Wolpert, Tom. *Whales for Kids*. Minocqua, WI: NorthWord Press, 1990.

Whitfield, Philip. *Oceans*. New York: Viking, 1991.

Wells, Susan. *The Illustrated World of Oceans*. New York: Simon & Schuster, 1991.

Ames, Lee J. *Draw 50 Sharks, Whales, and Other Sea Creatures*. New York: Doubleday, 1989.

Montroll, John and Robert J. Lang. *Origami Sea Life*. New York: Dover, 1990.

Livingston, Myra Cohn, editor. *If You Ever Meet a Whale: Poems*. New York: Holiday House, 1992.

Some Useful Addresses

The Whale Museum
P.O. Box 945
Friday Harbor, WA 98250

Center for Whale Research
1359 Smuggler's Cove Rd.
Friday Harbor, WA 98250

Pacific Whale Foundation
Kealia Beach Plaza, Suite 25
101 N. Kihei Road
Kihei, HI 96753

Friends of the Earth/Les Ami(e)s de la terre
251 Laurier Avenue, #701
Ottawa ON K1P 5J6

Save the Whales
P.O. Box 3650, Georgetown Station
Washington, DC 20007

Places to See Killer Whales

To see killer whales in the wild, take a cruise ship from Seattle in Washington's Puget Sound area. Or go to the Lime Kiln State Whale Watching Park on San Juan Island in northwestern Washington.

Where to See Killer Whales:

Marineland in Niagara Falls, Ontario

Marine World Africa USA in Vallejo, California

Miami Seaquarium in Miami, Florida

Sealand of the Pacific in Victoria, British Columbia

Sea World (California, Florida, Ohio, and Texas)

Vancouver Aquarium in Vancouver, British Columbia

Index

LAKE COUNTY PUBLIC LIBRARY
INDIANA

AD	FF	MU
AV	GR	NC
SEP 0 6 '95 BO	HI	SJ
CL	HO	CN L
DS	LS	

THIS BOOK IS RENEWABLE BY PHONE OR IN PERSON IF THERE IS NO RESERVE
WAITING OR FINE DUE.   LCP #0390